THE SUN BATHERS

THE SUN BATHERS

ROY MARSHALL

Shoestring Press

Printed by imprintdigital
Upton Pyne, Exeter
www.imprintdigital.net

Typeset by types of light
typesoflight@gmail.com

Published by Shoestring Press
19 Devonshire Avenue, Beeston, Nottingham, NG9 1BS
(0115) 925 1827
www.shoestringpress.co.uk

First published 2013

Cover image: *Sun Bathers*, 1932 by Leonard Beaumont
Linocut on paper, Museums Sheffield

Reproduced with kind permission from the family of Leonard Beaumont

ISBN 978 1 907356 85 8

ACKNOWLEDGEMENTS

Thanks are due to the editors of the following publications where some of these poems first appeared: *And Other Poems, Agenda, Antiphon, Cake, Critical Survey, Dream Catcher, Envoi, Frogmore Papers, Ink Sweat and Tears, The Interpreter's House, The Lampeter Review, Lighthouse, Magma, New Walk, Prole, The Rialto, Smiths Knoll, South, The North, The Shop, Stone Tide: William Soutar Prize Anthology 2011, The Ver Open Competition Anthology 2013.*

Some of these poems appeared in *Gopagilla* published by Crystal Clear Pamphlets 2012.

'Hawk's Eye' won third prize in the 2010 Ledbury Poetry Competition
'Da Vinci Packs For Pavia' was runner up in the 2012 Northants Poetry Prize
'Relic' won second prize in the 2012 Nottingham Open Poetry Competition
'The Bow Saw' was a runner up in The 2012 Alan Sillitoe Poetry Prize
'Student' won first prize in the 2013 Sheffield Hallam Universe Competition
'A Western Australian Piano Graveyard' was highly commended in the Ver Open Competition, 2013

Special thanks are due to John Lucas, to Rachel, Ian Parks, Rory Waterman and Jonathan and Maria Taylor for their advice and support.

CONTENTS

For Rachel and Alex

BLACKBIRD IN WINTER

He's on a branch above my head
velvet feathers at touching distance,
yellow ringed eye locked to mine.

Is an alarm call frozen in his breast,
the urge to fly curtailed by heavy air,
or is it to preserve energy and heat

that he keeps still? Can he sense in me
a lack of threat, recognise the need
to move slowly through slow air,

to sing a sub-song, out-live
short days by swallowing dark,
holding on to what light there is,

braced against the grip of a wind
unchallenged and un-breathed
since it skimmed down from the Urals?

RELIC

I'd rather take this road
to that chapel of larch on the hill

but my boy insists, so we step
into a nave of pines

screened by webs
where sound falls dead,

except for the rattle of cones.
Each breath is sealed with resin:

he finds a long bone,
lifts it from the needles:

fox or maybe badger, I tell him
taking his hand

suddenly aware
of our temporary skins.

ABROAD

We'd stayed too long, long after
the fire-wind and surfers had gone,
after our skins had begun to tell us
that we were near naked.

The sun drowned in waves
that all day crashed light into light
and now slid shadow
over shadow. The paperback

turned its pages; we hadn't noticed
the sea change its tune as we sank
and slipped over the dunes
to where gold turned to dust

and drained from our sandals
as it did from the heel of Talos
in that old Argonauts film. Now
our English winter made its presence felt;

petal-tender from the shower
you brought your stored heat to the bed
where cream-palmed I placed my hands
with all the lightness I could gather.

THE SUN BATHERS

They could be sisters with their matching bobs
and winter-white limbs; let's call them Dora
and Emily. Both warm-drowsy, both eighteen,
born on the eve of a war they're told
their fathers fought, although

in truth there's not much infantry can do
when faced with Howitzer, Maxim, gas
and wire. Dora's dad brought home shrapnel
under his skin and a deafening silence
except on nights when screams break free.

Emily's gazes from a mantelpiece;
he wears a peak that seems to her too big,
too shiny. In seven years this stretch
will be off limits, a sentry posted night
and day to scan air and sea, the pebble

slope a minefield, and none of us can say
who'll be a WAAF or WREN, working the land
or in a factory, nor if those nearby boys
will lob a ball and ask if the girls are free
for flicks at the Regal; nor if

by 1940, the long-limbed lads, let's call them
Bill and Johnny, will be gone as surely
as a night tide steals away the shapes
of bathing teenage beauties.

THINGS YOU SHOULDN'T TOUCH

The rotten wood wings of moths,
more delicate than powdered eyelids.

Vinyl grooves cut by kings of the blues,
hat brim thick in paper sleeves.

Illuminated manuscripts, thirsty
to drink from the whorls of your fingers

or the middle of negatives
carried down from the attic;

and before you hold to light
those amber strips of stilled life

first decide if your heart can take
what you'll find and what is missing.

STUDENT

The first of my many dead:
she washes, I dry,
dab his cheeks and lids,
change the water, roll him,
rub a sheet crease
from his back,
pat soft white buttocks,
take out catheter and cannula,
tape and press where blood
pools, thick as blackberry jam.

Julie's brisk, careful as a cook,
talks to him as if he could hear
and there's something in me
of the little boy, aproned,
allowed to help; his doughy-
ness perhaps, or the talc
like flour, as if this privilege
were a treat, the finished
parcel of taped sheets
something to be proud of.

NIGHT SHIFT

I've been reading in my break
how life and death are not separate
but as the Bhagavad Gita says

continuous. I go down to A and E,
wheel the patient into the lift
with a doctor and porter.

Upstairs, I'll push a shot of clot buster
through his cannula, hope he'll live
until hand over, that morphine floats him

to dawn. And the sun comes up as Becky,
in charge this shift, asks "How do you know
if you've found 'The One'?"

A WESTERN AUSTRALIAN PIANO GRAVEYARD

The farmer's pressing oil, olives spread
on mashing mats. We talk of chooks
and foxes, irrigation and bush fires.

I'm here to see ruins in meadows,
on outcrops, brought from sheds
and yards, lashed to utes and trucks.

"All good things return to earth."
She tells how a choral hum is raised
by strong wind, how possums nest in felt

and termites engineer collapse; how once
after rain, a derelict played like a pianola
as green tree frogs leapt in its heart.

I take her hand-drawn map, find
a Gold Rush era upright, laminate
blistered, keys jammed and gapped.

Despite its barroom look
a brass plaque by the keyboard
names an outback orphanage.

A Foley artist's dream, felt-less hammers
conjure horror from bass notes, or tap
a level crossing where the hero speeds

to make the gate. Each instrument
decays uniquely; a baby grand is legless,
veneer peeled like cherry bark.

Under cracked coffin-gloss
a clutch of white eggs.

CAREERS ADVICE

His beak dirty orange, the colour of seventies
sports car glass fibre, enveloped in my palm,
comfortable as a carved cane top.

I squeeze out the sponge, skim the sleek
sleeved neck, chase oily dreck from the down
of his chest. This one doesn't object, and this

we have in common; I dredge up the careers
officer as he plumped for tractor driving
while I sat and eyed him, mute as a swan.

ARM WRESTLING WITH NONNO

My mother told me how he altered
the river's course, how those muscles
were forged in the icy torrent where
he shifted boulders.

An alpine soldier of the first war,
later self-announced target
of Fascist batons and castor oil;
fireman, climber, hell-raiser.

I knew him in a wheelchair,
his demijohns of red turning
to vinegar under the stairs
as he sipped Orangina.

It was my face that brought light
to his pale eyes, and it was me
who, before he died,
he allowed to win.

UNCLE ALF, 1974

Licking a pencil to work out the figures
petrol consumption from gallons to litres

smart as a new pin in midday-sun,
off for cigars and an English paper.

First here thirty years ago
via Brixton, the desert, Monte Cassino.

ARRIVAL

Brush of stubble on peach, kisses planted
by sun-dried lips, Massimo in a vest
and me just six, climbing
from a Ford Escort onto a mountain.

The circuitry of crickets on air,
his red wine and cigarette breath,
a sickle and scythe laid aside,
and rosemary scent, rising.

The valley draped in wood-smoke webs,
my hair ruffled by his hardened hand,
the welcome I had never known till then,
when all the men of Italy loved me back.

CIMETERO

The gate kept a world out: scooters humming
along the road that ran down to the lake,
gellateria and monument.

Lizards froze, slipped into cracks, past photographs
set in granite, chrysanthemums on marble beds,
so different from the grassed churchyard at home.

I loved the honey heat, scent of rosemary
and privet, plots to walk between, adding dates
to calculate the ages of the dead.

One day, a grave, freshly dug, sides shored,
colour deepening from terracotta to crimson,
waiting not for Dad, who brought me here

because I asked, Dad, young and fit who'd live
forever, but for Nonno; next year, behind
polished glass, the face I'd know.

HAWK'S EYE

for Andy Green

Every grade and shape of manmade lens
is inferior to this; the quartz and amber set
that rests inside a kestrel's head

picks out the draught of moth wings,
the vales of a vole and low bellied furrow
of a cat snatching mayfly.

No wide angle will catch the breath that bows
a rabbit's flank or find a weasel's sine wave
through the geometry of plots.

No zoom will haul in a net of silverfish,
spot the printed silk of a butterfly's flit
or lift the blue-chrome of a fly's eye skyward.

No orbiting satellite will cleave a helix of gnats,
read the braille of ants across slabs or map
the reave of rats through a rice spill of larvae.

No mega pixel aerial photograph will trace a snail's
aluminium road, reveal the delta of a fox's spray
or catalogue a mouse's prey of grasshopper and louse.

A spy-plane won't find the mole's silo doorway,
pierce a pool's platinum skin, or read the swelled
camouflage of a frog primed for launching.

No lurid thermal image will capture the jolt
to the shrew's heart or the snatched plum
of its shadow rising beneath a drape of wings.

AUGUST 31ST, 1961

for Dilva

The sweating red-faced midwife,
a stern German stereotype,
says "push now" and "breathe deeply".

It is seven months since an offer
of Thalidomide, eight until
the Cuban Missile Crisis.

Ray Charles, headlining tonight,
is told to use the back door
of a club in Kansas.

In the hospital car-park in Surrey
our Dad is watching the moon rise,
already a target for Kennedy.

DYING ARTS

As the last window cleaner
born during the age of whistling
stashes his bucket and flannel

and millions of ear plugs play
into millions of closed circuit skulls
it seems the art is only practised now

by dry lipped ex-paperboys
in retirement homes
as they pour a morning brew

becoming as rare as thrush song
or the gaze of children
who sat silent and still

their eyes reflecting England
through the window of a train.

LEONARDO

I.   LA GIOCONDA

Da Vinci was amusing and witty, and on each day
that I sat he remarked upon my beauty.
And what was there not to smile about?

Francesco, who was rich with silk, had bolts brought to the Villa;
the olive of Tuscan hills spilt across my breasts and thighs,
the slopes of my hips and shoulders were the blue of Tuscan skies,

but the creased cream of clouds was only for his eyes, and yes,
I knew true happiness inside our frescoed walls.

Nothing that came after could temper my smile;
not my husband's death, nor life inside the convent,
not its cold crypt which the government demolished,

not obscurity nor fame before the cordoned crowd,
not the landfill beneath a green hill
where my bones lie ploughed.

II.   DA VINCI PACKS FOR PAVIA

Begin your list with *paper*;
you are always short of this.
White wax, charcoal, firestick.

Sketched skulls rest in margins,
brains trail fine-roots down the page
of your notebook. After *penknife*

and *spectacles with case*, a reminder
to steel yourself; *your stomach
may impede you. If not your stomach*

*fear of living through night hours
in the company of corpses,
quartered and flayed.*

More tools of the trade; *forceps,
fine-toothed saw, mirror, quills,
inkhorn.* Another shaded cranium

then notes, random and precise;
*obtain a head. Break the jaw
to see the uvula in place.*

Leave the house for wine and bread,
return to write *describe the tongue
of a woodpecker, the jaw of a crocodile.*

You remember the cold north, how your
hair tangles in the wind: so end with *comb,
a skin for the chest, towel, gloves, shoelaces.*

III.   LEONARDO IN THE MORGUE

Dogs and sundials are deep
in darkness. At this hour
only a cat moves, muscle
shifting under a loose coat,
the heart of a mouse ticking
in her jawbones.

On the marble slab
a peeled arm glistens.
This is no oil of duchess or duke;
it is all he can do to stop from puking.

Scalpel laid aside,
pencil blood-caked, cloth stretched
over mouth and nose, he'll draw
the limb from eight angles,
finish when the cock crows.

IV. ANATOMIA

The blade grips bone. Da Vinci sweats,
white dust on his cheeks and clothes.
One hand holds the skull
tight against the bench.

When finished he'll sketch
cavities and surface, a miscellany of teeth,
a side-panel of notes; for now
he'll make slow progress
through varnish and honeycomb.

At the keyhole, the wide eye
of a child, her jaw dropped
before the breathless flight home.

V.   PAVIA, 1510

*'CT scans have revealed that da Vinci's
anatomical sketches were startlingly accurate'*

Leonardo renders each layer
with an engineer's precision;
deep muscle ghosting strata
of tendons and sinew.

This, the drawing
you see before you.
This is *the* drawing.
This is you.

FLOODPLAINS

Between city edge and retail park
river and canal congregate.
Landlocked fields are lakes
after days and nights of rain.

How quickly landscapes are erased,
wind-throbbed fences become mute veins,
thistle and gorse turned
into loose aquatic weed.

Through an arc of wiper blades
miles of mirrored sky, only broken
by an island of horses
in a cloud of breath.

HARE

I find you on glossed stones
below the cliff, joints broken
at shoulder and haunch.

How did you come to be here,
bronze fur thick with clay-wash?
Were you coursed by river

to this open reach, or jump
into a full moon, sprinting
down a mirrored beam?

Sleek goddess who brings spring,
did you leave your form to outrun
hunters, were you christened 'Lust'

by a new creed, slip Boudicca's arms
before the thunderous charge,
divine our future in your leap?

THE CATCH

They came in summer, whole shoals flashing across
the dish of the moon, bound inland, breaking from waves
to skip shale and harbour walls, some snagged

on fences where they telegraphed the onrush of death
to uneasy farm dogs, others leaping hedges to rain
bullet-nosed onto bonnets,

gelid eyes smearing cracked windscreens
where drivers shook in dented wrecks,
lap deep in heads and tails,

while others hit the suburbs, poured through cat flaps,
dropped down vents to drown sleepers in basement flats,
splashed into reservoirs, guided by miles of pipes

to fly up between the legs of those making night visits
in sleeping Midland towns. We knew it would come to this;
we knew it as we laid our nets.

PEN

A flotilla slips from the water,
unusual in that the cob is absent.
Five cygnets stagger behind her
like air travellers leaving a conveyer
up a spattered bank
to sift and snatch at grain and bread.
She has an audience of novices,
her coterie and court; if not for these
she'd rise above the lake, span again
its breadth and length.

NO SIGNALS AVAILABLE

The sky is unmanned; no dash or scrape of vapour
in the high plateau of ghost ash, while grass on the hill
is flattened to gloss. These valley walls permit no signals,

but everything is in ceaseless discourse;
sparrows rip a double helix of midges, fish pluck skaters
from the skin of the lake, a gust helps me up the ridge.

Going home, hail falls hard on roof and windscreen;
you don't know this, but I am in love with you, as you move
through the purl of the city, un-tuned, as yet, to my frequency.

NATIONAL SERVICE

Smaller wars can be forgotten between wars:
afterward wars, the months and years of enforced peace.

A man of my Dad's generation told me how
you could go from Nissan hut and blancoed coal

to Korea in a week, how a lad might replace a sentry
shot that evening;

how at nineteen, you might catch shrapnel
in your spine and wheelchair bound

get home to find your teens at an end
and the swinging sixties just beginning.

SOUTHBANK

A helicopter flies low over the terrace
where a jogger dodges a group of kids,
all hair and skinny jeans, arms around
each other for a photo on a bench.

Parliament rises behind their peace signs,
the sun sets through spokes of the Eye,
a solitary Ray Davies stands and watches.
People kiss hello, pull chairs close,

glug wine into plastic cups, while a girl
in track-suit bottoms and a baseball cap
politely begs before she's moved on.
I'm thinking of Auden's

"poetry makes nothing happen";
but remember that letter, Brian Patten's
'The Stolen Orange' folded inside, how
it led to our marriage and child.

ROSE

For no good reason
we expected his Latin genes to colour him,

for a slick of black to crown him
as he emerged from between her legs;

for olive skin that would darken
at the touch of sun.

Tonight, feverish, pink cheeked,
mousy hair plastered on a milky brow,

he sleeps with her,
a small doppelganger

arms flung above his head,
a mirror of his mother.

Their murmurs and breath
float from open lips

his a perfect miniature
of her own sleep-slackened rose.

DANDYTIME

His gift to me,
the long-forgotten tempo
of a boy's life

as we stop
then start our way
along the old railway

snapping stalks, altering fates
as we go. Not a single clock
will be passed without being blown.

SPEED OF CLOUDS

The wind is revealed in the speed of clouds
in the stoop of air-bent conifers,
weighted and bowed like us my love,
braced, flexed, choice less.

RECORDS ON THE BONES

As kids we'd risk imprisonment,
pay our last rouble for contraband discs
pressed onto X-ray sheets,

grooves cut into opaque femurs,
hair-lined metatarsals and wrists,
furrows on fields of cranium, long since gone to ground.

Smuggled in coats though the streets
was the promise of jazz, sleeved between
twilight and heartbeat,

carried up back stairs to box rooms where
the snare flitted like sun-light through a line
of freight; this is how St. Louis and all its saints

came to Leningrad, in the bootlegged sound of those
who were born as slaves, musicians who drew us along
in the wake of all that western decadence.

JANET ARMSTRONG

listens to news from the Cape;
everything on schedule and A.O.K.

She drops a yolk into the flour,
wonders does anyone really know
if the surface will be as soft as this
or thin and fragile as shell?

Can anyone tell if his meringue
white suit will brown with heat,
if a helmet will leak like a pie lid?

She sings along to the radio
as another egg breaks:
"If I knew you were coming
I'd have baked a cake."

ARACHNOLOGY

Everywhere, except for the planet's poles,
they spill streams of progeny.

On shell-starred walls, above stone-floored
chapels, spinnerets and spigots bloom.

Hydraulic sprinter, rigger of hammocks
in abandoned cars, tattooist of dunes:

sometimes one will arrive between earth
and sky, to hang suspended between the two

and fondle air as if to check
an infallible hold over gravity.

VARNISH

The chauffer tells us to fold out the leaf
and take a look. There is a signature, pressed
into wood. Confetti in our hair, we wonder
if he wrote a cheque for a Savile Row suit.

Years later, I read of Archie Leach,
native son of Bristol, expelled from school,
told his mother had died
when she entered the asylum.

I imagine him in shades, a California tan,
window rolled down to sign for the fan
who waved as she clutched his autograph;
etched in varnish *Best wishes, Cary Grant*

OBREE AND THE HOUR

The bike you built won't let you down
unlike everyone else, so spine bowed
legs a blur, you're flying

as if pursued again by bullies after school,
tearing atmosphere that's clung too tight all your life.
Then it's gone; pain that this time you created.

Circle the boards once more,
come to rest awhile; slaps on the back
and handshakes won't hurt.

Tonight, for what it's worth,
the hour is yours.

*Cyclist Graeme Obree broke the record for the furthest distance travelled
in an hour in 1993. Obree, who suffered from bi-polar disorder and had
previously attempted suicide, rode a bike he had constructed from scrap metal
including washing machine parts. Obree's story is told in the film 'The Flying
Scotsman'.*

FLIGHT PATH

You get used to engines swallowing night air,
wide bodies smooth as whales and dolphins.

Cold slices my sleep through slates above the bed.
Our Southern Chicken uniforms hang

on the back of a chair. I imagine huge shadows
moving over the face of the moon,

orange burners glowing like the eyes of the big cat
Suah tells me that he saw in childhood.

"No-one in the village believed me but it was true.
And who can believe that people are up there

bound for another time zone. Like home,"
he murmurs. "Like home."

THE POSSIBLE FATES OF WREN'S GLOBE

Mare Tranquillitatis, Lacus Somniorum,
Lacus Mortis, Mare Vaporum …

Housed in a cabinet of curiosities,
sold at the Queen's request,
displayed by a renowned astronomer,
passed between inquisitive guests,

or elbowed from a spindle
in a Great Fire stampede
to become mosaic
in the London street,

or gathered dust
in a townhouse attic
to be blown into the sky
one night in the Blitz.

Any day a gardener's fingers
might smooth earth from the skin
of a moon fragment running
with tattoos of Latin.

CHESTNUT MARE

She bolted, gone with the saddle-harrow
still harnessed, the wild-haired boy
in chase across the field.

He found her later that evening,
broken legged by the van wheel, flank
heaving, eyes bulging

so the whites showed, and brought her
to the yard where days before
electric shears let her veins stand proud.

This time she shivers and shivers more
when the barrel is lifted
to her white blazed brow.

PRESENCE

And here too, in the place that loved you back,
your absence grows; in the guillotine of greenhouse
glass, in a trellis slung from the hips of a rose.
The sun hangs in an empty feeder which jigs and birls
on the cherry tree; a web spans tongue to heel across
your weather-cured shoes, still two sizes too big for me.

INHERITANCE

I'll take it now, that look you gave me,
the one I saw yesterday
as you passed an old man's hand
over an oak-framed table,

remembering how we lifted it from
a roof-rack and into family history
when I was twelve and you
were forty-seven.

All you felt and couldn't say was in
your steady gleam: I'll keep it with me,
like the knowledge that geese will return
to land beyond a screen of reeds.

I DREAMT OF SMOKING

the long abandoned sense of time
measured to a cigarette's length;
necessity and luxury, the sparked up camaraderie
of bus shelter, fire-escape, doorway in rain.

My dream wasn't a pining for breath given substance,
for jellyfish pulsing in a projector's beam,
not for rituals of unwrapping, tapping and rolling,
nor buried addiction, risen again.

But I know the source; it was you of course,
it was the two of us, smoking.

SEASON RINGS

Autumn, not spring
is the true beginning

when a floor is laid
in readiness

to feed shoots
and limbs.

We too must shed
small deaths

prepare to forge
new rings

from all our
fallen trappings.

THE BOW SAW

I'd go with Dad to the local woods,
collect fallen branches, the large ones
at a slant from his shoulder to mine,
our hands limed or browned by bark.

Across an up-turned tea-chest and held
by hand and boot, he'd saw through,
the pitch of blade-song dropping
as he reached the far side.

Older, I learnt the languages of wood:
dense oak coughing fine dust, jamming
the blade in the cut, asking more from
an aching arm, a racing heart and lungs;

soft hawthorn, torn by long strokes,
its give urging me on; but my favourite was pine
for its scent, first when cut, again
when burnt, the spittle-hiss

and crack as perfume stole the room.
It's years since the gas fire was installed
but on the garage wall hangs the bow saw,
handle faded, blade scabbed with rust

and blunt from use. I take it down
and I'm back in the woods, winter dusk
falling, our breath streaming out as we trudge
to the car, a branch span between us.

THE ARRIVALS

Two weeks after the neighbours left
he was back, a feline silhouette, distorted
in rippled glass, mewing for his usual saucer.

Ho Chi Minh, my mother called him,
and although she later claimed to dislike cats,
I remember how she tickled his milk damp chin.

The other arrival that spring was Vernon;
in tartan slippers, flares and vest, he'd walked
twelve miles to see my sister.

I remember the police car, how they palmed his head
as they eased him in, the posy of daffodils gathered
from a neighbour's garden, scattered in the road.

PROBABLY NOT THE BEST SUMMER JOB IN THE WORLD

Leave the sun to blaze on foyer doors,
scuff up stone steps, change into pink shirt
kipper tie, purple suit with wide lapels

climb behind a Perspex box, sell tickets
with grubby fingers, hand over Maltesers,
pop-corn, hot-dogs, ices,

get caught mid-impression by the manager,
an imitation of his voice hung like a jammed
frame in his stare,

mooch and ghost with dilated eyes
through drifts of smoke, blasts of *Pearl and Dean*,
muffled sobs, roller-coaster screams,

find lovers joined at the lips after the credits
have rolled, glide a banister to catch Michelle Pfeiffer
before she turns into a hawk,

exit via the fire escape to meet you for a quick half
between shows; apart from this last, no, I don't wish
I was back there, since you ask.

THE SECOND TEST

I never played; one either knew the unspoken rule
and came at season start with whites, pads, a bat,
or pulled on shorts and ran the track.

If the game is mentioned I have this shot to play;
a Long Room guest at Lords in '88, I saw
the legendary attack of Marshall, Ambrose, Walsh.

The truth; I drank too much to know who won the day,
and as we staggered to the tube, you in a birthright tie
and belted Mac, my sale-bought suit lost shape in the rain.

SILL

Nowhere better than this: half in,
half out of the house, looking up from a book,
legs stretched out behind glass or dangling
over slabs and grass, eyes full of clouds.

Watching a cat track a bird,
wondering where a vapour-trail ends,
stylus bobbing over the last few grooves
before its skim and lift.

Thinking of nothing, then of her,
waving to a neighbour who glances and grins,
sun spreading freckles on winter skin,
blood warm on one side, the other in shadow.

THE LESSON

"Out!" he yells, so we climb out
and stand on the edge, goose-bumped,
purple-lipped, some of us bird-boned,
xylophone-ribbed, others lank and broad,
muscling into manhood

and we wait in silence only broken
by teeth-chatter for the rest of the lesson:
punishment for diving straight in.
It's what I remember whenever
north wind meets wet skin.

AIM HIGHER

was the school motto.
Here's a picture that was never taken:

on the chapel roof with Bill, Andy and Tim,
feet braced against the gutter, cold arsed

in tight trousers and blazers, at risk
of expulsion, at risk of falling,

looking out across playing fields,
above us only sky.

SCHOOL

They're still here, brains
half-wired, in possession of knowledge
of how badly the world is run.

Bodies full of undiluted blood
carry folded tenderness and sex
that moves like white roots

through dreams dark as soil.
Their teeth gleam in un-diseased mouths
that worry the life from gum.

Their hair is sleeked
or sleep spun, holding heat
that sneaks through double glazing

to find them radiant
and dropping off mid-afternoon,
chins cupped in biroed hands that protrude

from pristine or grubby cuffs.
After all this time I recognise
boredom, unchanged,

like those thin static-hoarding jumpers
that will throw off sparks
when day's done.

WREN

Something frisks, drops
across my sight, stops in hawthorn's
wind-stripped fretting;
Wren, coin-size,
light-gleam held in your black-bead eye,
ruffled fellow traveller, gone
from my pilgrim path.

ZEN GARDEN

I trace the path of your spine,
slow at the lumbar rise,

stop at the crease
of your coccyx.

As the willow signs the pond
with the name of the wind,

as paper sips
from the brush's tip,

as bamboo bends
to the crane's wing,

so my breath will pass
over your skin,

send a ripple
to your heart,

set it
          darting.

LIVES OF POETS

Who
fondles bones
saw the ripple before he threw the stone
laid petals on your eyelids while you slept
steps unharmed from the avalanche's fist
is trapped in the amber of paperweight life
dives to find Excalibur but rescues a child
muffles the drum and amplifies the heart
draws out the thorn and holds it to the light
glimpsed himself hunted in the mist
listens for the signal of an intermittent god
writes with blood in the dust of a cell
is a butterfly resting on a wheel

WILFRED OWEN'S LAST LETTER

Death has taken leave; the cellar
so crammed night can't squeeze
under the low lintel of this forester's cottage.

He writes among the men, by a fire loaded
with damp wood. Pink cheeked, slack braced,
bare necked, they jostle and joke like factory boys

around a smoke, like miners at the bar
or navvies coming from winter cold, elbowing
and nudging in their rolled-up sleeves,

where the lid chatters on a pot and cards
are squarely dealt, a boy turns in the arms
of mothering sleep.

Low voices drift. He loves, he lives, he loves,
he lives. The beat in his temple, repeating this.

INSTANT KARMA

The office cleaner sings beautifully and in Hindi.
I ask her what her song means.

"The Lord says, I will give you what you want
when the time is right."

She leaves a world bright with belief,
the mopped floor under my feet,

the emptied bin of me.

CASE

I finger-walked a map last night,
took a dotted line before the sun focused its heat,
past the artillery range, under an arc of ghost ordnance
into absent sea, the beach brow furrowed,
tide-times biroed on my hand.

The sound of guns once reached this coast,
carried on the wind from France.
The phone in my shirt knocks my chest with each step,
slender as the cigarette case in the town museum
that kept a bullet from a soldier's heart.